Women Empowerment In India: Past, Present And Future

:: Author ::

Dr. Ketaki Sheth

Associate Professor

Anand Commerce College, Anand

PUBLISHED BY

HEMCHANDRACHARYA INTERNATIONAL PUBLISHING HOUSE

H.Q AT & POST-CHAVELI, TA-CHANSMA,

DIST-PATAN NORTH GUJARAT, INDIA, ASIA

www.iphouseindia.com

Claims to copyright in published and unpublished books or manuscripts can be registered as literary works in the Copyright Office. Textual works with or without illustrations are eligible, as are other no dramatic literary works, including fiction, nonfiction, poetry, contributions to collective works, compilations, directories, catalos, dissertations, theses, reports, speeches, bound or loose-leaf volumes, pamphlets, brochures, and single pages containing text. This contain may be also help to web site and Wikipedia this contain at also available to books See sl-35, *Registering a Copyright with the U.S. Copyright Office*, for the methods available for copyright registration

First Publication: 15TH December, 2016

Women Empowerment In India: Past, Present And Future

Copyright: Author

(c) **Dr. Ketaki Sheth**

ISBN:- 978-1-54523-003-9

Price: Rs. 800/- INDIA
       $ 15 OUTSIDE INDIA

PUBLISHED BY

HEMCHANDRACHARYA INTERNATIONAL PUBLISHING HOUSE

H.Q AT & POST-CHAVELI, TA-CHANSMA,

DIST-PATAN NORTH GUJARAT, INDIA, ASIA

www.iphouseindia.com

Preface

Entire 21st century has been devoted for the upliftment of women throughout the world. Women are equally competent on all social, economic, political ,religious, sports and administrative fronts. This book on **"Women Empowerment In India: Past, Present and Future"** is a modest attempt in this direction to give a spark to powerful, prospective, emerging women in India.

The book is divided into six chapters on various issues related to women empowerment. Chapter one is related with 21st century Indian women. Chapter two discusses about ICECD(International Centre For Entrepreneurship and Career Development). This centre is acatalyst for Women Entrepreneurship. Chapter three describes women contribution in peace, purity and plenty in our society. Chapter four states that pink colour is not next to anybody. Chapter five is devoted to women education, earning and empowerment. Chapter six explains the policies and practices related to women entrepreneurship.

This book is an addition to already existing literature but from different angle and vision. Author hopes that the book proves to be value addition to all students, scholars and professors. Author is highly thankful to Hemchandracharya International Publishing House, At & Post-Chaveli Ta-Chansma Dist-Patan for accepting the manuscript and bringing out it in valuable book form.

Dr. Ketaki Sheth

INDEX

SR.	CONTENT	PAGE NO.
1	21st Century Women in India	1-15
2	ICECD: An Ever Shining Star on Local And Global Scenario	16-30
3	Women Empowerment: From Peace to Plenty	31-39
4	Women Entrepreneurship: Pink Color Entrepreneurship in India.	40-55
5	Women Empowerment: From 3K's to 3E's	56-67
6	Women Entrepreneurship : Policies and Practices	68-84

21ᵗʰ Century Women in India

INTRODUCTION

THE ANCIENT VEDAS STATE: "YATRA NARI PUJJNTE, RAMANTE TATRA DEVATA" this means wherever women is respected, God resides there.

Late Prime Minister Shri Jawaharlal Nehru has rightly said, "You can tell the condition of nation by looking at the state of its women". This paper throws light on: whether women empowerment in India is just an illusion or empowered Indian women are a symbol of strength and are marching ahead towards pride, peace, purity and plenty.

Empowerment is the process of awareness, capacity building leading to greater participation, greater decision making power, controlled and transformative action. Women empowerment means an increase in strength of women such as spiritual, political, social or economic. The term women empowerment does presuppose the existence of self-esteem and self-confidence. It emphasis on 3 E's namely education, earning and empowerment.

Rashtrapita Mahatma Gandhi has rightly said "If you educate a man, you educate an individual, but if you educate a woman, you educate an entire family."

Empowerment of women has become the topmost national and international concern in 21st century. Government initiatives alone are not enough. Society must assure that there is no gender discrimination. women should enjoy sense of equality on all social, economic, political, sports and business fronts. Women all over the country should remember that "empowerment cannot be given to you on a golden platter, if should come from within" We should remember that "The very spelling SHE includes HE, HE does not include SHE" Indian women do realize that there is long way to go but at the same time they are hopeful: "WE SHALL OVERCOME".

FACTS AND FIGURES

Globally speaking the statistics suggested by UN highlight and bring forth some shocking facts, such as -

- 70% of the 1.2 billion people living in poverty are female.
- Women do more than 67% of hours of work done in the world and earn only 10% of world's income.
- They own only 1% of the world's property.
- Women are paid 30-40% less than man for comparable work on an average.
- 60-80% of the food in most developing countries is produced by women.
- Women hold between 10-20% managerial and administrative jobs.
- 60% of the 130 million children between the age group of 6-11 years, who do not go to school, are girls.
- Approximately 67 % of the world's 875 million illiterate adults are women.

IMPORTANT DIMENSION OF WOMEN EMPOWERMENT

The empowerment of women is a contemporary issue regardless of country in which social planner tries to bring us sustainable development. Though women empower me-nt is not sufficient condition it is still a necessary condition in order to stabilize and in turn to have sustainability in the development process. Empowerment is now increasingly seen as process by which one gets, power with and power within. Some defined empowerment as a process of awareness conscientization, of capacity building leading to greater participation, effective decision ma king power and control leading to transformative action. This involves ability to get what one wants and to influence others. With reference to women the power relation that has to be involved includes their lives at multiples levels, family, community, market and the state. Importantly it involves at the psychological level women ability to assert them and this is constructed by the "gender roles" assigned to her especially in culture which resist change like India. Women in different societies are always been portrayed in different manner and women especially in context to Indian society have always been an instrument of pleasure and thus has remain a piece of mockery this paper seeks to examine the status of women keeping in mind the present situation.

The following are important dimensions of women empowerment: The government of India declared 2001 as the year of women's empowerment (Swashakti). The national policy for the empowerment of women was passed in 2001. UN has declared entire 21st century for upliftment of women throughout the world. Some qualities to be acquired by women to become truly empowered are political, legal, economic, and health awareness. They should have knowledge about support group and positive attitude towards life. They should get goals for future and strive to achieve them with courage. The best gift parent today can give to their daughter is education. If women choose to be ignorant then all the efforts taken by the government and women activists will go in vein. Even in twenty-fifth century, they will remain backward and will be paying a heavy price for the dependence, so, it is wake up call for women to awake from that deep slumber and understand the true meaning of their empowerment.

GENDER EQUALITY

Gender equality plays a crucial role in uplifting women. Rather, gender inequality certainly needs to be abolished. Gender based discrimination and disparity are evident from various dowry cases and sexual harassment incidents. The idea of equal employment opportunities is still lingering unimplemented in several remote areas. Women in some accessible areas are yet confining to their household routines while their spouses go for work. India has the lowest percentage of women employees (23%), followed by Japan (24%), Turkey (26%) and Austria (29%), according to the corporate gender gap report brought out by the world economic forum. Women should be given freedom to choose their interest of work and discharge their duties: unbiased Government should open its door for women to give opportunities to prove themselves at par with men.

The principle of gender equality is enshrined in the Indian constitution, in its preamble, fundamental right, fundamental duties and directive principles. The constitutions not only grants equality to women, but also empower the state to adopt measures of positive discrimination in favor of women. Empowerment is the one of the key factors in determining the success of development in the status and position of women in the society. We put a special focus on empowering women and girls, because we believe they hold the key to long lasting change in communities. Empowering women must be a united approach, a cause that requires continued attention and stewardship by all. We need to augment our efforts for empowering women and enhance their progress. It is our moral, social and constitutional responsibility to ensure their progress by providing them with equal rights and opportunities. Today women with their smartness, grace and elegance have developed on fronts. They with their hard work and sincerity have excelled in each and every profession. Women are considering being more honest, meticulous and efficient and hence more and more companies prefer hiring women for better performance and results.

- **Health and education:** Women empowerment can be achieved chiefly through health and education. "Health is wealth" basic sanitation facilities, adequate medical camps, government health schemes would be conductive to bring about a major change. Enrolment of girls in schools makes huge difference in transforming the nation.

- **Important decisions:** In the 21st century, women enjoyed more freedom and power than ever before. However, they are still at disadvantage when compared to men in virtually all aspects of life. Women are deprived of equal access to education, healthcare, capital and decision making power in the political, social and business sectors. Increased income controlled by women gives them self-confidence, which helps them to obtain a voice and vote in:

- House hold decisions such as domestic well being decision. For instance, women tend to use income clout for more equitable decision about sons and daughter diet, education and health.

- Economic decisions: acquiring, allocating and selling assets.
- Fertility decision: economically empowered women tend to have fewer children.
- Land use and conservation decisions: rural women tend to favor sustainable environmental practices since they are usually the one's that collect the families natural resources such as water and fire wood.
- **Economic empowerment:** Female economic power also enhanced the "wealth and well being of nations." Women who control their own income tend to have fewer children, and fertility rate have shown to be inversely related to national income growth. Women are also more able- and generally more willing than male counterparts- to send daughter as well as sons to school, even when they earn less than men. in turn, a women's level of education affects her decision making process when it comes to question about contraception age of marriage, fertility, child mortality, modern sector employment and earnings. But women's economic empowerment must not

be examined in vacuum. The intersection of political, social / cultural and environmental conditions must be analyzed. Factors impacting women's economic empowerment include:

- Violence: women are the predominant victims of conflicts, sexual violence, injury, death, intimidation and human trafficking.
- Lack of access to education, training and technology
- Lack of access to clean water, sanitations
- Lack of access to responsible health care/ reproductive health (one of the cost of widely available pre-natal screening in India has been the selective abortion of female fetuses,
- Lack of access to credit/ finance, safe work conditions, living/ minimum wages
- Cultural practices, traditions, religious interpretations of women status
- Women's lack of knowledge about rights and laws (economic, social, political, religious)

- Lack of adequate representation in decision making procedure and governance structure.

WORKING WOMEN AND CHALLENGES

Working women in India are faced with lot more challenges than their counter parts in the other parts of the world. In India men do not share on most of the household chores. It is women, who have to cook, clean the house, do the dishes, wash clothes, get their children ready for school etc. men just took care of few chores that are to be dealt to be outside the house. So the major burden of running the family is on the shoulders of women. With the house hold work on one hand and the official work on the other hand, this double burden has made their life hectic.

- **Relationship with Colleagues:** Although women are employed in each and every sector, they face certain problem working among the male counterparts. As we live in patriarchal society so men try to dominate women even though she is capable and hardworking. Men think twice in promoting her to higher post. As women are mostly of co-operative nature they try to co-operate with their opposite and try to deal with the situation calmly. There are certain male who prefer themselves among women and if a women is succeeding they envy her and try to dominate her.

- **Health Problems:** Women taking care of household work at the same time have to look after the official work. This double burden has made their life hectic. A large number of women worker complain of headache, back pain, circulatory disorder, fatigue and mental disorders. Poor nutritional status anemia due to poverty and cultural practice where women eat last and increase work load due to domestic responsibilities, lead to fatigue among women. A large number of women workers complain symptoms such as a irritability, moods swing, depression, sadness and constrictions problems. Women working in some industries like construction, brick lines, electronics industries etc suffer from gynecology problems, miscarriage, premature deliveries etc and give birth to babies with low birth weights and birth defects.

- **Lack of basic facilities:** Lack of basic facilities like toilets, rest room, dining space etc at the work place cause a lot of physical discomfort and mental stress decides leading to several urinary tracts and other diseases, particularly among pregnant women.

- **Time management:** Working women have a dual responsibility i.e. official works and responsibilities of house hold works hence it becomes difficult for them to manage their time. They have to take care of their children, cook food and at the same time look after the management of the office. Moreover women who are married find it difficult to cope up with this stress. They have to listen to her husband, his need, and her children and at the same time work hard at the office. This is the basic reason why most women leave their job and prefer to stay at home and take care of their family.

- **Sexual harassment:** In 1997, the supreme court of India, for the first time, recognized sexual harassment at the work place as a violation of human rights. The Supreme Court in Visakha and other v. state of Rajasthan laid out certain guidelines which imposed a duty of co-workers towards their female employees. The guidelines place the responsibilities on employers to provide a safe work environment to their women employees and include both preventive and remedial measures to make work environment safe for women employees, in this context the supreme court introduced the "The Protection of Women against sexual harassment at work place bill 2010".

CONCLUSION

Empowerment of women has become the topmost national and international concern in 21st century. Government initiatives alone are not enough. Society must assure that there is no gender discrimination; women should enjoy sense of equality on all social, economic, political, sports and business fronts. Women all over the country should remember that "empowerment cannot be given to you on a golden platter, if should come from within" We should remember that "the very spelling SHE includes HE, HE does not include SHE" Indian women do realize that there is long way to go but at the same time they are hopeful: "WE SHALL OVERCOME"

REFERENCES

- AIR 1997 Supreme Court 3011
- Desai Vasant ," Entreprenurial Development and Small Business ", Himalaya Publishing House, New Delhi.
- Gupta and Srinivasan "Entreprenurial Development" S. Chand Publication Mumbai.
- National Policy- http:// en.Wikipedia.org/wiki/women_in India.
- M. Eswari, "Problems faced by the working women in the era of Globalisation.

ICECD: An Ever Shining Star on Local And Global Scenario

Introduction

We live in an era where "SURVIVAL OF THE FITTEST" (Spencer's phrase) is of extreme importance. In 2016, second decade of 21st century, women are no longer related only with three P's (namely pickle, powder and papad) they are no longer related only with three K's (namely kids, kitchen and knitting). Women are aptly related with three E's namely educator, earning and empowerment. This is above ICECD (International Centre for Entrepreneurship and Career Development) plunges into the picture for women empowerment since 1986 right born local upto global scenario.

ICECD and Hina Shah are two sides of the same coin. Hina Shah is founder director of ICECD. This is a heart-felt story of "A Dream Comes True" how an energetic and visionary lady transforms her into on entrepreneurship **come** alongwith the development of globe, overcoming the barriers of geography, age and creed.

This is a true story of how a catalyst like Hina Shah transforms herself from a simple Master of Science into a legendary social entrepreneur alongwith developing ICECD and thousands of deprived, poor and helpless women around her allover the globe.

Hina Shah, a Master of Science with specialization in Human Resource Development areas faced many an odds when she decided to become an entrepreneur after completing her MSc. At that time, society (be it parents, husbands, in laws, relatives, neighbours, banks or even market) was not prepared to see women being independent. However, with determination and grit to achieve her goal she emerged a successful entrepreneur in the field of plastic packaging, while effectively balancing various other roles of a mother, a wife and a daughter. Gradually, she received acceptance from family and society.

While having experienced problems and constraints

herself, when she came across deprived, poor and helpless women suffering due to economic deprivations, it disturbed her. She decided to take up the mission to lead them towards self - employment and entrepreneurship. She pioneered. "Women Entrepreneurship Development Programmes" in Ahmedabad, Gujarat, India - in 1982, with 25 women participants of which 16 established their non - traditional businesses. Encouraged by the success she refined the model and implemented it in other districts of Gujarat and various states of India. These women entrepreneurs were recognized as "economic contributors" by the financial /support institutions and the policy makers, and specialized women development policies were formulated by the government to support women in rural areas.

Her concern for these women suffering translated into a dream to expand this movement to the disadvantaged and poor women in nook and corner of the rural areas of the country. To do this, she felt the need to build up a specific national / international level organization, with no limitations or defined boundaries to work for these women. Thus, in 1986 she started "The International Centre for Entrepreneurship and Career Development" (ICECD). ICECD is a unique institute for entrepreneurship; perhaps the only one of it is kind that has facilitated thousands of disadvantaged women and youth to become entrepreneurs not only in India but all over the developing world. It came to be recognized as a Centre of Excellence by the United National ESCAP Thailand in the year 2000.

HINA SHAH – in her own words…

"My vision continues to be THE ECONOMIC EMPOWERMENT OF WOMEN, but the final mission is the achievement of FULL EQUALITY and TOTAL ALROUND DEVELOPMENT of WOMEN. My efforts will culminate only when women from all strata of the society, particularly the disadvantaged and the poor, will achieve a sense of overall empowerment through meaningful participation and decision making at family, community and policy levels.

Our Women Empowerment Strategies have tapped powerful reservoirs of hope and enthusiasm among women who used to view themselves negatively. This empowerment process starts with changes in consciousness and in self perception of women. This has been the most explosively creative, energy releasing transformation, one from which there is no looking back.

I perceive a very positive and vibrant future for the women of India. They will enjoy better status in family, community and society as well as in the professional field. We have successful women role models, who have proven that they have the capability to succeed in any given field, be it politics, economics, or social sphere.

In future, I see myself having reached out to every woman of India, realizing my dream of seeing these women as independent decision makers, entrepreneurs and socially and economically empowered in the true sense."

HINA SHAH – TITAN BE MORE LEGEND 2010

Hina Shah was chosen as the TITAN Be-More Legend 2010 by the people of India. Titan company, with its philosophy of "be more" set out for a "search for explorers" to identify people who actually lived to their fullest. From amongst a thousand life explorers; people who believe they weren't born to live just one life, Ms. Hina Shah, was chosen the TITAN Be-More Legend 2010.

ICECD and Women Entrepreneurship model for villages

ICECD believes in the irreversible empowerment approach through capacity building. The institute periodically examines social and economic situations, analyses needs and finds ways to bridge the gaps. This has brought effective learning and behavioral changes, enabling women to carry out functions independently and effectively. ICECD through its trained manpower has also developed volunteers/SHG leaders and Area Development Officers (ADOs) who were trained and developed to monitor and look after their group members. They created a local handholding facility, which proved to be a fantastic strength for these women whenever a difficulty arose.

The rural women who at times worked as agro-labourers for generations, when pressed by economic need, had no access to alternative economic opportunities to rise above poverty.

ICECD targeted these women and slowly empowered them by sensitizing, motivating, training and developing them to become economically independent by linking them with the dairy business, its promotion, creation and management; linking them with ICECD micro-credit support and to other financial institutions, thus facilitating them towards investment and capital formation through dairy and other house hold businesses; providing them with technical training for dairy business, besides other businesses like garment making, food processing, spice making, cattle feed, etc.

Iyava Vasna model has been replicated in about 30

villages of Gujarat among other states in the nation, and in Asian and African countries. The aim is to replicate the model to 50 more villages in Gujarat in coming years.

ICECD has been able to implement an irreversible process of development in the society at large whereby it has benefited the disadvantaged women who have been able to overcome the physical, financial, psychological and social sufferings. This is ICECD's tribute to humanity and the society.

ICECD and Women at Local Governance

Most of the women elected in Local Governance at the village level are not educated, thereby lacking exposure or specific leadership skills. ICECD works to build leadership and vision amongst these women leaders for effective functioning through :

- Advocacy and awareness building for women rights and opportunities
- Creating awareness about roles and responsibilities of elected women in local self government

- Creating counseling cell to support women leaders
- Education and capacity upgradation of village heads/"women sarpanch" towards need-based socio-economic empowerment of villages
- Building of specific skills of women sarpanch to discharge their duties effectively.

More than 230 women political leaders (Sarpanchs and Panchayat leaders) have been trained by ICECD in various districts of Gujarat.

ICECD and Science and Technical Women Graduates

Many women with science and technical background have realized the need for entrepreneurship, however the non-availability of professional courses for enterprise management is the bottleneck they face.

ICECD has taken up the challenge to offer such

training courses based on its experiences of developing entrepreneurs over the last two decades. So far, the centre has already conducted several Entrepreneurship Development programmes for women with Science & Technology background – at national / regional level with the support of National Science and Technology Entrepreneurship Development Board (NSTEDB) and the Indian Ministry of Science and Technology.

In the context, ICECD has developed specific approaches and training modules to initiate and enable successful enterprise development amongst these graduate women.

The course contents are continuously updated, including the instruction material – as per the development taking place at global standards.

The centre has trained over 500 women (Science & Technical Graduates) who have started successful business with investment over Rs.10 million, in fields like Automobiles, Electrical Appliances, Chemicals etc.

ICECD and Handicapped Women

Under ICECD's Garment Skill Upgradation programme, specific training is conducted for Apang Manav Mandal, wherein physically challenged girls are trained to manufacture various types of garments. 35 handicapped girls were initially trained. Conducted technical skill upgradation training in garments for other men and women.

The participants gained knowledge of garment manufacturing, designs & fashions, and the new opportunities / technology / machines and its application in the garment industry

The Achievement motivation module helped the participants to gain self-confidence, calculated risk taking ability, communication skills and behavioural competencies

58 Young women have started their own enterprises earning between Rs.20,000 – Rs.30,000 per month and the rest work in textile industries with salaries ranging

between Rs.5,000 – Rs.25,000 per month.

Women empowerment through e-learning is not outside the scope of ICECD. ICECD has setup e-learning centers with fully developed infrastructure and these centre are handed over to women SHGs in the community. They have been trained to manage the centers and carry video-conferencing successfully.

ICECD and Future Map

The reach of ICECD has extended to lakhs of marginalized rural/tribal women of 21 districts of Gujarat, namely Ahmedabad, Surendranagar, Sabarkantha, Mehsana, Gandhinagar, Bharuch, Anand, Patan, Navsari, Surat, Kheda, Vadodara, Kachchh, Banaskantha, Dahod, Junagadh, Valsad, Panchamahal, Rajkot, Amreli and Jamnagar. This successful experience was then expanded and replicated by ICECD by developing other NGOs and grassroots organizations all over India (in over 19 states of Rajasthan, Madhya Pradesh, West Bengal, Bihar, Andhra Pradesh, Tamil Nadu and Karnataka, among others).

The successful stories of Women Economic Empowerment became an inspiration to other developing nations, and the team at ICECD became instrumental in initiating and institutionalizing Women Entrepreneurship Development in countries like Zambia, Bangladesh, Lesotho, Botswana, Cameroon, Malaysia, Philippines, Jordan, Sri Lanka, Guyana, Ivory coast, St. Kitts, and many others spanning the continents of Asia, Africa, Pacific and the Caribbean.

The multiplier effect of ICECD's endeavors has reached more than 60 developed/developing countries of Asia, Africa, Caribbean and Pacific regions, with over 1150 organizations and 5500 plus trainers having been trained in the international arena.

Conclusion

ICECD and Hina Shah are something more than CATALYSTS.

(By the way, catalyst is chemical substance which itself does not take part in chemical reactor but makes speedier the reaction by its mere presence). ICECD and Hina Shah have transformed themselves into path-breaking institute and towering personality alongwith allround development of thousand of deprived women allover the globe. It is our common experience that manytimes government initiative and resources do not give us expected result. In such disappointing and discouraging environment, an NGO like ICECD has worked wonders. Achievements and concrete performance of ICECD and Hina Shah are not less than a MIRACLE.

WOODS ARE LOVELY, DARK AND DEEP

BUT ICECD HAS PROMISES TO KEEP

MILES TO GO, MILES TO GO

ON AN ENDLESS VOYAGE.

Let no all try Y for women empowerment (alongwith ICECD and Hina Shah) positively so that all women overcome barriers of caste, color, age, creed and make empowered their families, society, nation and world at large through proactive and successful social entrepreneurship.

References

1. Entrepreneurship development by Vasant Desai, Himalaya Publication House
2. www.icecd.org

Women Empowerment: From Peace to Plenty
A POEM FOR YOUR REFLECTION:

We had our first argument last night, and he said a lot of cruel

things that really hurt me.

I know he is sorry and didn't mean the things he said, because he sent

me FLOWERS TODAY.

I got FLOWERS TODAY. It wasn't our anniversary or

any other special day.

Last night he threw me into a wall andstarted to choke me.

It seemed like a nightmare, I couldn't believe it was real

I woke up this morning sore and bruised all over.

I know he must be sorry because he sent me FLOWERS

TODAY.

I GOT flowers today, and it wasn't Mother's Day or any

other special day.

Last night, he beat me up again, it was much worse than

all the other times

If I leave him what will I do? How will I take care of my

kids?

What about money? I am afraid of him and scared to leave.

But I know he must be sorry because he sent me FLOWERS TODAY How do you help someone like this?

- ❖ **Faces of Indian Women**

    One of the most enduring clichés about India is that it is the country of contradictions. Like all clichés, this one too has a grain of truth in it. At the heart of the contradiction stand Indian women: for it is true to say that they are among the most oppressed in the world, and it is equally true to say that they are among the most liberated, the most articulate and perhaps even the most free. Can these two realities be simultaneously true?"

    Urvashi Butalia

- ❖ **Facts about India**

    Largest democracy in the world

    Land boundaries with Bangladesh, Bhutan, Myanmar, China, Nepal and Pakistan

Area: 3,287,590 sq.km (slightly more than one-third the size of US)

Coastline: 7,000 k.m.

Population: 1,065,070,607 (Growth rate of 1.44%)- second largest population in the world

Sex ratio: 1.07 male (s)/female

Life expectancy at birth: 63.25 years (male) and 64.77 years (female)

Ethnic groups: Indo-Aryan 72%, Dravidian 25%, Mongoloid and other 3%

Religions: Hindu (81.3%), Muslim (12%), Christian (2.3%), Sikh(1.9%), Others (2.5%)

Languages: 18 major languages; 216 languages in total and several thousands dialects

Literacy: 59.5% (total population); 70.2% (male); and 48.3% (female)

❖ **Place of women in Indian society:**
A (cultural) historical perspective

➢ The Goddess (*Devi*)

➢ The mother

- The sister
- The wife
- The *daughter*

❖ **Indian Women in Modern Times**

Education

- Gender gaps in higher education
- About 1 percent of total women population has college education
- Women account for a third of the students at college/university level
- In engineering and business, the proportion of female students is much smaller
- In education, nearly half of the students are women

❖ **Indian Women in Modern Times**

Barriers to Female Education

- Poverty: one-fourth of India's population lives below the poverty line (2002)
- Social values and parental preferences
- Inadequate school facilities

- Shortage of female teachers: 29 percent at the primary level and 22 percent at the university level (1993)
- Gender bias in curriculum

❖ **Indian Women in Modern Times Employment**
- Difficult to get an overall picture of employment among women in India
- Most women work in the informal sector
- Women accounted for only 23 percent of the total workers in the formal sector in 1991
- The number of female workers has increased faster than the number of male workers
- Female unemployment rates are similar to male unemployment rates

❖ **Indian Women in Modern Times Barriers to Female Employment**
- **Cultural Restrictions**
  - Hierarchical society (caste system)
  - Purdah system: the veiling and seclusion of women
- **Discrimination at Workplace**

- More prevalent in fields where male competition is high
- Less prevalent in fields where competition is low
  - **Lack of employment opportunities**

❖ **Indian Women in Modern Times**

Empowerment

▲ Social Empowerment

- **Education**
  - There is no direct relationship between education and work force participation; but may affect their participation in household decision making
- **Economic Independence:**
  - Economic independence does not imply significant improvement in social standing
  - Culture and tradition play an important role
  - A small fraction has opened up towards Western values

❖ **Indian Women in Modern Times**

Economic Empowerment

- **Property Rights**

- Patriarchal society
- **Economic Decision Making**
  - In the household
  - In businesses

❖ **Indian Women in Modern Times**

Political Empowerment

- Representation in democratic institutions
- Government reservations policy for women: the constitutional amendment of 1990s

❖ **TRIVIA**

- Recognize Famous Faces

- ❖ Famous Faces
  - ➢ Indira Gandhi
  - ➢ Mother Teresa
  - ➢ Mira Nair
  - ➢ Kalpana Chawla
  - ➢ Gurinder Chadha
  - ➢ Arundhati Roy
  - ➢ Jhumpa Lahiri
  - ➢ Aishwarya Rai
  - ➢ Sushmita Sen

- ❖ **Introspection**

  Faces of an Indian woman
  - ➢ Wife

- Mother
- Sister
- Bread earner
- Compassionate member of the society

"The origin of a child is a mother, a woman. ….she shows a man what sharing, caring, and loving is all about. That is the essence of a woman."

Sushmita Sen, Miss Universe 1994

…but that is just a beginning….

Refrences:

Desai Vasant, "Entrepreneurial Development and Small Business" Himalaya Publishing House, New Delhi

Gupta ans Srinivasan, "Entreprenurial Development"S. Chand Publication, Mumbai

M. Eswari, "Problems faced by the Working Women in the era of Globalisation"

Women Entrepreneurship: Pink Color Entrepreneurship in India.

Introduction:

Spirit of enterprise makes man an entrepreneur. Entrepreneurship is nothing but creative and innovative response to environment.

According to government of India "woman entrepreneur or pink color entrepreneur is an entrepreneur who owns and controls a business unit, brings at least 51% capital from her sources and gives at least 51% job opportunities generated in the unit to woman".

Woman Entrepreneur Category

Women in organized 86 unorganized sector

Women in traditional 86 modern industries

Women in urban 86 rural areas

Women in large scale and small scale industries.

Single women and joint venture.

Categories of Women Entrepreneurs in Practice in India

First Category

Established in big cities

Having higher, level technical & professional qualifications –

Nontraditional Items

Sound financial positions

Second Category
Established in cities and towns

Having sufficient education

Both traditional and non-traditional items

Undertaking women services-kindergarten, crèches, beauty parlors, health clinic etc.

Third Category
Illiterate women

Financially week –

Involved in family business such as Agriculture, Horticulture. Animal Husbandry, Dairy,, Fisheries, Agro Forestry, Handloom, Power loom etc.

Women Entrepreneurship in India

States	No of Units Registered	No of Women Entrepreneurs	Percentage
Tamil Nadu	9618	2930	30.36
Uttar Pradesh	7980	3180	39.84
Kerala	5487	2135	38.91
Punjab	4797	1618	33.77
Maharashtra	4339	1394	32.12
Gujarat	3872	1538	39.72
Karnataka	3822	1026	26.84
Madhya Pradesh	2967	842	28.38
Other States & UTS	14576	4185	28.71
Total	**57452**	**18848**	**32.82**

Challenges Woman Entrepreneurs in India

The financial institutions are skeptical about the entrepreneurial abilities of women. The bankers consider women loonies as higher risk than men loonies. The bankers put unrealistic and unreasonable securities to get loan to women entrepreneurs. According to a report by the United Nations industrial Development Organization (UNIDO), "despite evidence that women's loan repayment rates are higher than men's, women still face more difficulties in obtaining credit, often due to discriminatory attitudes of banks and informal lending groups (UNIDO, 1995b)

Another argument is that women entrepreneurs have low-level management skills. They have to depend on office staffs and intermediaries, to get things done, especially, the marketing and sales side of business. Here there is more probability for business fallacies like the intermediaries take major part of the surplus or profit. Marketing means mobility and confidence in dealing with the external world, both of which women have been discouraged from developing by social conditioning. Even when they are otherwise in control of an enterprise, they often depend on males of the family in this area.

Women's family obligations also bar them from becoming successful entrepreneur in both developed and developing nations. "Having primary lit home and older dependent family members, few women can devote all their time and energies to their business" (Starcher, 1996). The financial institutions discourage women entrepreneurs on the belief that they can at any time leave their business and become housewives again. The result is that they are forced to rely on their own savings, and loan from relatives and family friends.

Knowledge of alternative source of raw availability and high negotiation skills are the basic requirement to run a business. Getting the raw materials from different souse with discount prices is the factor that determines the profit margin. Lacks of knowledge of availability of the raw materials and low-level negotiation and bargaining, skills are the factors, which affect women entrepreneur's business adventures.

Finally high production cost of some business operations adversely affects the development of women entrepreneurs. The installation of new machineries during expansion of the productive capacity and like similar factors dissuades the women entrepreneurs from venturing into new areas.

Low-level risk taking attitude is another factor affecting women folk decision to get into business. Low-level education provides low-level self-confidence and self-reliance to the Women folk to engage in business, which is continuous risk taking and strategic cession making profession. Investing money, maintaining the operations and ploughing back money for surplus generation requires high risk taking attitude, courage and Confidence. Though the risk tolerance ability of the women folk in opposite to that, day-to-day life is high compared to male members, while in business it is found opposite to that.

How to Develop women Entrepreneurs in India

Better educational facilities and schemes should be extended to women folk from government part.

Adequate training programme on management skills to be provided to women community.

Encourage women's participation in decision-making.

Vocational training to be extended to women community that enables them to understand the production process and production management.

Skill development to be done in women's polytechnics and industrial training institutes. Skills are put to work in training-cum-production workshops.

Training on professional competence and leadership skill to be extended to women entrepreneurs.

Training and counseling on a large scale of existing women entrepreneurs to entrepreneurs. Remove psychological causes like lack of self-confidence and fear of success.

Counseling through the aid of committed NG0s, psychologists, managerial experts and technical personnel should be provided to existing and emerging women entrepreneurs.

Making provision of marketing and sales assistance from government part.

To encourage more passive women entrepreneurs the Women training programme should be organized that taught to recognize her own psychological needs and express them.

State finance corporations and financing institutions should permit by statute to extend purely trade related finance to women entrepreneurs.

Women's development corporations have to gain access to open-ended financing.

The financial institutions should provide more working capital assistance both for small scale venture and large scale ventures.

Making provision, of micro credit system and enterprise credit system to the women entrepreneurs at local level.

Industrial estates could also provide marketing outlets for the display and sale of products made by women.

A Women Entrepreneur's Guidance Cell set up to handle the various problems of women entrepreneurs all over the state.

District Industries Centers and Single Window Agencies should make use of assisting women in their trade and business guidance.

Programmers for encouraging entrepreneurship among women are to be extended at local level.

Training in entrepreneurial attitudes should start at the high school level through well-designed courses, which build confidence through behavioral games.

More governmental schemes to motivate women entrepreneurs to engage in small scale and large-scale business ventures.

Outstanding Women Entrepreneurs
Mrs. Keerti Deshpande-Amod Consultants

Mrs. Keerti Deshpande has completed her B.E in Mechanical Engineering from Government College of Engineering, Aurangabad having proprietor ship business of valuation of movable and immovable properties, providing techno economical viability study assistance

Her firm undertakes jobs for all types of industries, from packaging to paper mill, from flour mill to sugar factories, process industries like distilleries and petrochemicals related industries.

She has been working for evaluation of assets of a few municipal corporations. She is looking forward to get a good work experience with some big brands for mergers and acquisitions. She has completed her assignment for an educational trust. That was a good achievement for her. Her goal is to be the most experienced in her field.

Specialties: Plant & Machinery Valuation, Asset Register preparation 8 maintenance, Chartered Engineer, Transmission Line Surveys, TEV study

Mrs. Yogita /Unit Nahar- Amyo Technologies

Mrs. Yogita is engineer by profession. She has completed her engineer branch of electronics and telecommunication from S.S.V.P.S.C.O.E, Dhult, Currently. She is running Amyo Technologies which is situated at T-5, STPI, MIDC, Chikalthana. The company is working in information technology (L.T) industry since last eight years. Earlier Mrs.Yogita was working as a project manager in e-Gain communications; pune which is a US based multinational company. Then she has decided to do something which was to be created by her own and the idea struck in her mind that to go for making of ERP software as she was having good experience of software industry, Initial investment for this business was an office and only 10 computers.

She is having sole proprietorship for this business, currently working as founder and managing director of Amyo Technologies Pvt. Ltd. there are total 50 engineers working in this company from customer support, development, testing and marketing team. Majorly focus on the production of educational ERP known as "Shikshan Kranti". Mrs. Yogita first generation entrepreneur and she has awarded with the Best IT Company for Government of Maharashtra'.

Dr. Vaidehi Wakte-VW Foods

Dr. Vaidehi is organic chemist by profession. She has completed her education from Akola she has completed M SC organic chemistry from akola and recently completed with her PhD in organic chemistry.

She is of 35 years old and running the food industry which mainly deals within chocolate and confectionaries.

Recently January 2013 she has started with this business name as VW foods. She is having one outlet in CIDCO, shop no. 13 Ellora complex, Connaught place, Aurangabad.

As the business is very new, it's in the infancy stage she is haying only 5 employees in her industry. The chocolates are completely handmade along with the chocolate VW chocolates Food also produce certain confectionery items. Within very short period of time the chocolate bouquets from the store got famous at in city.

Smt, Snehal Dantale- Dynasound

She has completed masters in home science from Anek College, yawatmal. Earlier she was housewife but after the death of her husband she got involved in the business. And now also Dynasound is providing service throughout the Maharashtra.

When her husband started this business initially he has started with only 1000 Rs. and no worth turnover of the business is near about 60 lacks per annum. In Marathwada only Dynasound is having the hanging system of martin brothers company which is having unique features and very important for their work.

Dynasound since from 1993 has provided the sound system for more than 5000 programs throughout the Maharashtra. In every year they provide the service for Aurangabad Ellora Festival which is one of the very famous events in Aurangabad every year.

Dynosound also provided the service in entertainment programs like in concerts of Late. Bhimsen Joshi, Pandit shivkumar Sharma. Pandit Hariprasad Chaurasia, Pandit Jasraj,Ustad Rasheed Khan, Gulam Ali, Anup Jalota. Udeet Narayan and many more celebrities.

In 2012 Smt. Snehal was awarded with Gaurav Puraskar by Gagruti Manch, Aurangabad she was also awarded by Shambhu Raje puraskar. She is presently on election committee of Shishu Vihar Vidya Mandir, Aurangabad.

Mrs. Aditi Someshwar

Aditi Someshwar is an engineering graduate who initially worked in Pune and Mumbai, but had to move to

Aurangabad when she got married.

After a three year break due to motherhood. She felt the urge to start working again and began teaching at a government college. It wasn't long though before she wanted something more. This led to the setting up of Wiztel, a training firm in 2008. Networking helped her to sign up as a franchisee with Vedang Radio Technology Limited. She now trains and places engineers in this company. Naturally, her company met with a lot of wariness, but today, Aditi feels that setting up such a business in a small town has worked well for her.

Her business was self funded and what drove her was the desire to stay in line. She enjoyed while being able to manage the home front. Her business is expanding rapidly and she is now looking at tapping into the local industry in Aurangabad for projects. Her advice to future Entrepreneur.

Conclusion:

Entrepreneurship especially women entrepreneurship improves health and wealth of family, society and nation.

Women now a day's captured many fields which were considered domain of man in past. They have proved that they are second to none. There contribution in economic growth is praise worthy, pink colour entrepreneurship should be designed in such a way that it meets the challenges of local, national and global markets women entrepreneurs do have competence to sustain and strive for excellence in dynamic environment posed by liberalization, privatization and globalization.

References:

1. Desai Vasant, Dynamics of Enterpreneurship Development and Management, Himalaya Publishing House, Mumbai
2. Gupta Srinivasan, Enterpreneurship Development, Sultan Chand & Sons, New Delhi.
3. Prof. Rushink Khan, Prof. Raman Karde, Sachin Gaikwad, Women Enterpreneurship and Economics Development: A Case Study of Marathwada Region, Proceding of International Conference on Transgenerational

Enterpreneurship Economy and Innovation Dynamics for Sustainability.

4. Tankodara Jagdish P, Women Enterpreneurship Development in India, Proceding of International Conference on Transgenerational Enterpreneurship Economy and Innovation Dynamics for Sustainability.

Women Empowerment: From 3K's to 3E's

Introduction:

The term Women Empowerment does not mean only specific activities but it is a process through which women can raise their voice for needs and interests the purpose is to make women independent to take any decision of her life, Society and personal development. It aims at making them independent from all social family and professional limitations. All treatments towards them should be through to an end. This is very essential for the development of the nation. Encoveraging women in all fields are an utmost priority of the nation. Gender inequality should be considered as social evil training programmes and conferences should be held to make them self reliant. This will ultimately lead to active and better society.

Women and Education

Only those women have created the history who are highly educated. In india the literacy rate of women is lesser than a man. As according to the survey of 2011, the literacy rate of man is 82.14% whereas the literacy rate of women is only 65.46%. The same literacy rate (64.13) was of man in 1991. So we can say that the women are somewhere two decades back in progress. Well, a consolatory thin is the literacy rate of woman is rising and the difference between man-woman literacy rate is descending.

The literacy rate of women in 1951 was only 8.86% which is now 65.46%. it can be a notable progress. The man-woman literacy difference was 18.3% in 1951, 25.16% in 1961, 23.98% in 1971, 26.62% in 1981, 24.84% in 1991, 21.69% in 2001 and 16.68% was in 2011. Thus the difference between man-woman literacy rates is diminishing especially after 1981.

Participation of Woman in Work

Women do 60% household works and 98% domestic work. She performs duties like; cooking, cleaning, and raising children, caring for old age people or other people which are avoidable in present accounting system. 70% women work at unskilled professions and hence earn little. Women work more 6 hours than man but her work has lesser value. Out of total working hours, 60% belong to women but she is the holder of only 1% property of total international property.

The responsibility of children stops her from joining from current flow, the fear of absorption and discrimination, lesser facilities of information and mass media, less education and the disbelief that woman is for domestic and household work are possibly the reasons of her lesser income).

Woman and Health

In many families woman and girl becomes the victim of the ill-health and she suffers from anemia and suffers from an unhealthy body. It is important to have motherhood and it is a precious gift from nature to the woman but unfortunately it proves to be a harmful for a woman in India. Only 42% deliveries are done under the moderation of a doctor. Majority women appoint local midwives during pregnancy. As a result of lacking tools and a proper skill/it becomes difficult to save a mother in critical situation during the delivery. India is at second number on the deaths occurring during pregnancy. According to the report of this also affects the health of a woman. Domestic UNDP 88% women are lacking the balancing of nutrition. Moreover the minor works (like, cleaning and the use of traditional gas) harm the health of a woman. Report of UNISEF says that 22% women bear motherhood before the age of 18. 40% underage marriages occur in India and 22% women bear motherhood at the age of only 22).

Woman and Political Participation

The survey of `Sansadeyparishad' in around 100 nations, women are the leader of only 10% political parties. There is almost 50% man and 50% woman in the society but in the parliaments of India there are less women leaders than men.

In the first parliament in 1952, there were 4.4% (22) women. It is yet below 10% till 14th parliament. Recent parliament has 61 (50 more than first) members are elected. Comparatively the result is poor and the same is in other parliaments of states.

In 1995, the chairperson of 11th parliament, Nazamaaheptulla had presented the, proposal for the 33% allocation for women on the international women's day and it W^{as} accepted but before it applied, the parliament was destroyed and it remain unapP^1,^{1}e":$_s$ Recently the 15"1 parliament has passed majority span but no signs can b$_e$ seen of its application. There are 33% allocated seats for women in state level institutes, so that can enter into the politics from a little step but at the same time it is also true women are not tend to participate from village level.

Sincere steps for women Empowerment

The crimes related to women must be stopped so that the fear of insecurity can be removed. The application of the rules must be done properly.

It is importance to her work. Though lesser women hold the top status but the way the girl students are shining in different courses of education, we can say they have equal IQ with man.

To ignite self confidence in woman so that she must be aware towards her rights.

She must be independent economically. The proper steps towards applications or programs and protection for the wages discrimination can be done. Moreover a woman must be more skillful. Thus she will get more income and improve her economic status.

To break those thoughts which cannot respect women, government must give proper support to the helpless woman.

Woman Empowerment in Economic Field

The woman working in traditional professions has improved her condition through this program. Women are trained for 35 different skills like repairing computer, electronic watch, radio and television. For the development of woman "Svaya.mSeedhaYoja.na. (2001.)" is applied; the main aim of this program is the development of woman. For that Self Help Groups are formed.

'SakhiMandals' are established under this program. Many attempts are done for the economic empowerment of woman yet we have not got expected results and woman has become the victim of double responsibility. 2/3"1of total working hours belong to women but they earn only 10th part of total income. Women contribute in half share of production. Yet only 100th share of farming belongs to woman. Majority of land belong to man. There are 1/3rd of women in labor yet they are given the works of lesser wages. The top positions are hold by only 2% of woman. There are only 13% to 20% women. The participation of woman is ignored. Indian society has given less attention to the woman.

Woman Empowerment at family field:

She is given economic rights like; she is earning now, she has right to prepare budget and make shopping, woman education has improved and she has a right to vote and can take part in politics but she is not considered completely equal to man in the family. The discrimination of son and daughter is more or less there in the society. The abortion of girl child and domestic violence happens in the society. She does not have complete right on her income. Religion, orthodox thoughts and values are responsible for the familial empowerment of woman. As a daughter she is standing in the middle. She can see the bright future if she looks in future but if she looks back she can see the orthodox society making her existence useless.

Woman Empowerment in Legal Field:

'Diwani' and 'Fojdari' laws. Help woman for marriage and legacy. It protects -woman from different violence like; rape, kidnapping, prostitution, cruelty, physical absorption etc. But these two rules are not enough. Some more rules are formed, for example; 1) The downy prohibition act, 1961 is erected in 1968; 2) pre-mature prohibition act is erected in 2006; 3) the recent law of protection of woman from domestic violence. Many other laws were applied to empower woman. As Margaret Alva says, the status of woman in law is highest in India than other nations. Theoretically many attempts are done to empower woman. But practically she is not in a condition to use these rights because of ignorance, rituals, traditions etc. Our Indian constitution provides the unique status to the woman, but because of the social, economic and religious incapability, women remain at the secondary position.'

Woman Empowerment in Education:

SarvaShikshaAbhiyan started in 2001 in which the removal of imbalance of man-woman literacy rate is under focus. `Kasturba Gandhi BalikaVidhayalayYojana' is for girls of ST, OBC, and backward class and for minority which provides them shelter. This program is applied where a girl has to leave her study because of long distance to her school. `MadhayanBhojanYojana' is applied to force children to continue their study and provide them healthy food. Thus even poor parents have started to send their girls to school. `MahilaSamanyyojana' is for the empowerment and education for limited social groups. In these programs, they try to spread awareness, equal rights for status of the woman. Presently this program covers 21,000 villages of 102 districts of 10 states. Moreover some other programs are `Rashatereey Maadhayamik Shiksha Abhiyan (2009-10)',`Proth sikshan and saakaar bharat, mafat kanya kenvani, scholarship, kishori Shakti yojana (2001) and because of those programs, the rate of woman education has increased but equality between man-woman education cannot be seen. The literacy rate in man has increased from the beginning. In 20U1, the literacy rate in man was more than 75% whereas it was less than 54% in woman. In 2011, the literacy rate in man is more than 87%, the woman has it less than 70%. Thus during 60 years, literacy rate has increased but as compared to man it is yet lower than our expectation. In 2011, more than 29% woman is illiterate.

Conclusion:

Woman in India has progress a lot, much has been accomplished a lot is yet to be achieved. 3K (Kids, kitchen, Knitting) are matter of past. Similarly 3P's (pickle, powder and papad) are also past phenomena. At present Indian Woman are closely related with 3E's namely Education, Earning, and Empowerment. Entire 21st century is devoted for upliftment of women as rightly declared by UN.

References:

1. Desai Vasant, Dynamics of Enterpreneurship Development and Management, Himalaya Publishing House, Mumbai
2. Dr.Minaxi P Jethwa (2014), International conference at Christ Institute of Management, Rajkot.
3. Dr.Sanjay Pandya(2014), International conference at Christ Institute of Management, Rajkot.

4. Gupta Srinivasan, Enterpreneurship Development, Sultan Chand & Sons, New Delhi.

WOMEN ENTREPRENEURSHIP: POLICIES AND PRACTICES

DEFINITION OF WOMEN ENTREPRENEUR BY GOVERNMENT OF INDIA:

According to Government of India:-

"Woman Entrepreneur is a person who…

(i) Owns and controls a business unit,

(ii) Brings at least 51% of capital employed in the unit from her sources. And

(iii) Gives at least 51% of jobs generated in unit to women".

❖ **TIPS ON HOW TO MAKE YOUR BUSINESS COME TO LIFE**

- Do a Self Inventory
- Develop an Idea
- Test the feasibility and location
- Write a business plan
- Identify your market
- Determine the cost & establish a budget
- Find the right investors and listen to investors
- Set – up a great support system
- Determine the legal structure
- Select and register your business name

- Take advantage of free resources
- Determine tax obligations, secure permits and licenses
- Set up books of account
- Share ideas with your friends and family and be flexible
- Consider positive criticism
- Maintain quality of product and services
- Be patient (Cool and Calm)/Don't worry about dilution/don't fear the competition
- Network
- Provide outstanding services to your customers
- Time management
- Know that honesty is the best policy
- Have balance in your life (Work life balance)

❖ WOMEN OWNED MICRO-SMALL AND MEDIUM ENTERPRISES IN INDIA: AN OVERVIEW

MSMEs in India are broadly divided into two classes according to the Provisions of the MSME Development (MSMED) Act, 2006

These are

➢ Manufacturing enterprises engaged in the manufacturing or production of goods pertaining to any industry specified in the first schedule of the Industries Development and Regulation Act, 1951, defined in terms of investment in plant and machinery.

➢ Service enterprises engaged in providing or rendering of services defined in terms of investment in equipment.

❖ **Definition of micro, small, and medium enterprises based on investment**

Type	Manufacturing (investment in plant and machinery) Indian rupees million ($ thousands)	Service (investment in equipment) Indian rupees million ($ thousands)
Micro	Up to 2.5 (Up to 45.5)	Up to 1.0 (Up to 18.2)
Small	2.5 – 50.0 (45.5 – 909.1)	1.0 – 20.0 (18.2 – 363.6)
Medium	50.0 – 100.0 (909.1 – 1818.2)	20.0 – 50.0 (363.6 – 909.1)

❖ **MSMEs' access to finance**

Funding source	Share (percent)

Formal financial sources	21.50
Self-equity	3.30
Informal sources	75.00

Sources: Annual Report of Ministry of Finance 2012 Annual Report of Ministry of Micro, Small and Medium Enterprises 2012.

❖ **CLASSIFICATION OF WOMEN-OWNED MSMES**

Category	Registered	Un-Registered	Total	Total versus all women-owned businesses (percent)	Total versus all MSMEs (percent)
Micro	274,059	2,655,318	2,929,377	97.62	9.40
Small	40,722	30,414	71,136	2.37	0.23
Medium	276	-	276	0.01	0.01
Total	315,057	2,685,732	3,000,789	100.00	10.25

Prevalence of women-owned businesses	State-wise Share (percent)	Number of states/union territories (#)	States/union territories	Combined share (percent)
High	>10.00	4	Kerala, Karnataka, Tamil Nadu, West Bengal	51.9
Medium	5.00-10.00	2	Andhra Pradesh, Madhya Pradesh	11.5
Low	2.00-4.99	7	Rajasthan, Maharashtra, Punjab, Uttar Pradesh, Bihar, Gujarat, Odisha	26.7
Very Low	<1.99	20	Rest of India	9.9

Sources: Annual Report of Ministry of Finance 2012 Annual Report of Ministry of Micro, Small and Medium Enterprises 2012.

❖ **GEOGRAPHICAL DISTRIBUTION OF WOMEN-OWNED MSMES**

Sources: Annual Report of Ministry of Finance 2012 Annual Report of Ministry of Micro, Small and Medium Enterprises 2012.

❖ **ACCESS TO FINANCE OF WOMEN-OWNED ENTERPRISES**

Funding source	Share (percent)

Formal financial sources	3.1
Semi-formal financial sources	4.8
Self, family, friends or informal Sources	92.1

Sources: Annual Report of Ministry of Finance 2012 Annual Report of Ministry of Micro, Small and Medium Enterprises 2012.

❖ SUPPLY OF FINANCE TO WOMEN-OWNED MSMES BY DIFFERENT INSTITUTIONS

source	Financing supply share (percent)
Public sector banks through microcredit	30
Public sector banks to small scale industries	38
Prime Minister's Rozgar Yojana	2
Swarna Jayanti Shahari Rozgar Yojana	1
Swarna Jayanti Gram Swarozgar Yojana	4
Private sector banks	19
Foreign banks	5

Sources: Annual Report of Ministry of Finance 2012
Annual Report of Ministry of Micro, Small and Medium Enterprises 2012

❖ GOVERNMENT SCHEME FOR WOMEN-OWNED MSMES

➢ **The government has an ambitious 14-point action plan for public sector banks to increase women's access to bank finance, including MSME finance.** It set a target of 5 percent aggregate public sector bank lending to women and instructed the central bank to track performances. Following this, Reserve Bank of India (RBI) in 2000 asked public sector banks to report credit extended to women. This resulted in an increase of loans to women from **2.36 percent in 2001 to 5 percent of total lending in 2007.** Aggregate net bank credit to women increased to 6.3 percent in 2009, with 25 banks reaching targets.

➢ Apart from MSME-specific initiatives, **India's 11th five-year plan encourages ownership rights for women by offering incentives for registration of property.** Women homebuyers benefit from tax exemptions, lower stamp duties, and easier availability of home loans. This could help women who own MSMEs to get greater access to collateral and, in turn, access business finance.

❖ GOVERNMENT SCHEME FOR WOMEN-OWNED MSMES

➤ **The MSME ministry has flagged the promotion of women-led enterprises as a key priority area.** In 2008, the ministry launched the government of India's only financing scheme for women entrepreneurs. However, lack of awareness among target clients led to low uptake of this scheme. In 2012, loans of Indian rupees 7.7 million ($140,000) were disbursed against a target of Indian rupees 38 million ($700,000).

❖ GOVERNMENT SCHEME FOR WOMEN-OWNED MSMES

Scheme	Implementing Agency	Details	Features
Trade Related Entrepreneurship Assistance and Developme	Ministry of Micro, Small and Medium Enterprises	Objective is to provide better access to finance. non-governmental organizations	Credit: 30 percent of total project cost as government grant, 70 percent by the

nt (TREAD) scheme for women		to be the implementing agencies by lending funds to entrepreneurs	appraising institution Training and development: Indian rupees 100,000 for the NGO conducting the program

Sources: Annual Report of Ministry of Finance 2012
Annual Report of Ministry of Micro, Small and Medium Enterprises 2012.

❖ **Role of DIC (District Industries Centre)**

➢ Different schemes of government of Gujarat for overall development of the state.

➢ The procedure for starting business is same for men and women. Following are the different schemes published by Government.

➢ Schemes for MSME

1. Vyaaj Sahaay
2. Gunvatta Sahaay
3. Skill development schemes
4. Market development schemes

5. Award scheme for best MSME

❖ **Schemes for Cottage Industry**

➢ Shri Vajpayee bankable scheme

➢ Prime Minister's employment generation programme

➢ Jyoti Gram Vikas Yojana

➢ Maanav Kalyan Yojana

Address of DIC: 213-215, Jilla Seva Sadan, Near Borsad Crossroad, Anand Phone/Fax: 02692-260865, 264372

Important link: http://www.imd-gujarat.gov.in/schemes/01-002.html

❖ **OUTSTANDING QUALITIES OF WOMEN ENTREPRENEURS**

Some of the Outstanding Qualities of Women Entrepreneurs are:

Accept Challenges	Ambitious
Drive	Enthusiastic
Hard Work	Patience
Passionate	Motivator
Skillful	Conscious

Keenness to learn and imbibe new ideas	Perseverance
Intelligent	Determination to excel
Devotion	Experienced
Ethical Behavior	

❖ PROBLEMS BEING FACED BY WOMEN ENTREPRENEURS IN INDIA

- Poor self-image of women
- Inadequate motivation
- Discriminating treatment
- Work-Life Balance
- Role conflict
- Cultural values
- Lack of courage and self – confidence
- Lack of social acceptance
- Lack of freedom of expression
- Afraid of failures and criticism
- Lacking in leadership qualities
- Time Management

References:

Desai Vasant, "Entrepreneurial Development and Small Business"

Himalaya Publishing House, New Delhi

Gupta ans Srinivasan, "Entreprenurial Development"S. Chand Publication, Mumbai

M. Eswari, "Problems faced by the Working Women in the era of Globalisation"

Refrences:

Desai Vasant, "Entrepreneurial Development and Small Business"

Himalaya Publishing House, New Delhi

Gupta ans Srinivasan, "Entreprenurial Development"S. Chand Publication, Mumbai

M. Eswari, "Problems faced by the Working Women in the era of Globalisation"

Refrences:

Desai Vasant, "Entrepreneurial Development and Small Business"

Himalaya Publishing House, New Delhi

Gupta ans Srinivasan, "Entreprenurial Development"S.

Chand Publication, Mumbai

M. Eswari, "Problems faced by the Working Women in the era of Globalisation"

Refrences:

Desai Vasant, "Entrepreneurial Development and Small Business"

Himalaya Publishing House, New Delhi

Gupta ans Srinivasan, "Entreprenurial Development"S. Chand Publication, Mumbai

M. Eswari, "Problems faced by the Working Women in the era of Globalisation"

Refrences:

Desai Vasant, "Entrepreneurial Development and Small Business"

Himalaya Publishing House, New Delhi

Gupta ans Srinivasan, "Entreprenurial Development"S. Chand Publication, Mumbai

M. Eswari, "Problems faced by the Working Women in the era of Globalisation"

Refrences:

Desai Vasant, "Entrepreneurial Development and Small

Business"

Himalaya Publishing House, New Delhi

Gupta ans Srinivasan, "Entreprenurial Development"S. Chand Publication, Mumbai

M. Eswari, "Problems faced by the Working Women in the era of Globalisation"

Refrences:

Desai Vasant, "Entrepreneurial Development and Small Business"

Himalaya Publishing House, New Delhi

Gupta ans Srinivasan, "Entreprenurial Development"S. Chand Publication, Mumbai

M. Eswari, "Problems faced by the Working Women in the era of Globalisation"

Refrences:

Desai Vasant, "Entrepreneurial Development and Small Business"

Himalaya Publishing House, New Delhi

Gupta ans Srinivasan, "Entreprenurial Development"S. Chand Publication, Mumbai

M. Eswari, "Problems faced by the Working Women in

the era of Globalisation"

Refrences:

Desai Vasant, "Entrepreneurial Development and Small Business"

Himalaya Publishing House, New Delhi

Gupta ans Srinivasan, "Entreprenurial Development"S. Chand Publication, Mumbai

M. Eswari, "Problems faced by the Working Women in the era of Globalisation"

Refrences:

Desai Vasant, "Entrepreneurial Development and Small Business"

Himalaya Publishing House, New Delhi

Gupta ans Srinivasan, "Entreprenurial Development"S. Chand Publication, Mumbai

M. Eswari, "Problems faced by the Working Women in the era of Globalisation"

Refrences:

Desai Vasant, "Entrepreneurial Development and Small Business"

Himalaya Publishing House, New Delhi

Gupta ans Srinivasan, "Entreprenurial Development"S. Chand Publication, Mumbai

M. Eswari, "Problems faced by the Working Women in the era of Globalisation"

Refrences:

Desai Vasant, "Entrepreneurial Development and Small Business"

Himalaya Publishing House, New Delhi

Gupta ans Srinivasan, "Entreprenurial Development"S. Chand Publication, Mumbai

M. Eswari, "Problems faced by the Working Women in the era of Globalisation"

Refrences:

Desai Vasant, "Entrepreneurial Development and Small Business"

Himalaya Publishing House, New Delhi

Gupta ans Srinivasan, "Entreprenurial Development"S. Chand Publication, Mumbai

M. Eswari, "Problems faced by the Working Women in the era of Globalisation"

References:

Desai Vasant, "Entrepreneurial Development and Small Business"

Himalaya Publishing House, New Delhi

Gupta ans Srinivasan, "Entreprenurial Development"S. Chand Publication, Mumbai

M. Eswari, "Problems faced by the Working Women in the era of Globalisation"